MW00616249

TRAINING
YOUR THINKING

TRAINING YOUR THINKING

21 Days of Mental Discipline

by Rick Hawkins

Copyright © 2017 – by Rick Hawkins

Publisher—eGenCo

All rights reserved. This book is protected by the copyright laws of the United States of America. This book may not be copied or reprinted for commercial gain or profit. The use of short quotations or occasional page copying for personal or group study is permitted and encouraged. Permission for other usages must be obtained from eGenCo or the author. Unless otherwise noted, THE HOLY BIBLE, NEW INTERNATIONAL VERSION®, NIV® Copyright © 1973, 1978, 1984, 2011 by Biblica, Inc.® Used by permission. All rights reserved worldwide. Scripture taken from the New King James Version®. Copyright © 1982 by Thomas Nelson. Used by permission. All rights reserved. Unless otherwise indicated, all Scripture quotations are taken from THE MESSAGE, copyright © 1993, 1994, 1995, 1996, 2000, 2001, 2002 by Eugene H. Peterson. Used by permission of NavPress. All rights reserved. Represented by Tyndale House Publishers, Inc. King James Version is recognized in most of the world, as well as the United States, as public domain.

Powered by eGenCo   Generation Culture Transformation
Specializing in publishing for generation culture change

eGenCo
824 Tallow Hill Road
Chambersburg, PA 17202, USA
Phone: 717-461-3436
Email: info@micro65.com
Website: www.micro65.com

facebook.com/egenbooks   youtube.com/egenpub

egen.co/blog   instagram.com/egen.co

twitter.com/egen_co

Publisher's Cataloging-in-Publication Data
Hawkins, Rick.
Training Your Thinking. 21 Days of Mental Discipline.
by Rick Hawkins
72 pages cm.
ISBN: 978-1-68019-862-1 paperback
     978-1-68019-863-8ebook
     978-1-68019-864-5ebook

1. Christianity. 2. Daily Devotional. 3. Mental Discipline.
I. Title
2017905329

Interior layout by Versatile PreMedia Services, Pune, India.

I would like to thank my son, Dustin Hawkins, for his assistance in writing this book.

Table of Contents:

Introduction

Have you ever asked yourself the question, *"Why am I the way I am?"* To answer this question you must ask yourself, *"Why do I think the way I think?"*

These questions are not only legitimate, but are also keys to finding paths and patterns to a better way and style of living. Many people are locked into a way of life that they do not question. There is either the feeling that there is nothing wrong with their patterns or the feeling that they do not have the ability to control or change them. Nothing could be further from the truth!

Everyone can change his or her life. Change happens by first recognizing that there may be a need for change. Once that is determined then you must ask, *"What needs to change and how do I change it?"*

We are all, in most part, a product of our thinking. According to the twenty-third Proverb, *"...as he thinks... so is he."*[(1)] To help you grasp the significance and seriousness of your thought process I will introduce you to the practice, the product and the power of right thinking. A man who is familiar with the effect and potential impact of this triad is someone who is established in his identity.

As you read through this devotional over the next twenty-one days and apply these principles and practices of mental discipline to your life, you will begin to see your purpose flourish and enjoy fulfillment in every area of your life.

Let's get started!

DAY 1:

Thoughts Precede Reality

There is potential within every seed. The potential the seed carries is not completely dependent on the seed itself, but more so on its surroundings and how it is handled. The seed's exposure, atmosphere, environment and soil have everything to do with the seed's ability to produce.

Think of thoughts as seeds. The same principles that apply to seeds are at work for thoughts. When a seed is placed in the correct environment, atmosphere and soil it does not remain a seed. In the same way, a thought does not always remain a thought. Thoughts carry great potential just as a seed does. You must practice handling thoughts properly. If a thought lacks the environment to unlock its intended potential, that thought will remain dormant: a lifeless and buried seed.

Think about this—you were a thought before you were a reality. You were in the mind and heart of God before you were a life form in your mother's womb. You must KNOW and BELIEVE that you are NOT an accident. God told Jeremiah, *"Before I formed you..., I knew you."*[1] There was a certain fabrication that transpired in God's mind before He made that fabrication manifest. It is powerful to realize where you came from! This realization helps you to understand your projected course—where you are going and how you are getting there.

How did God's thought turn into a reality? He spoke what He was thinking! God said, *"Let us make man in our image."*[1] That *"image"* produced a thought. That thought, in turn, became words. The spoken words became a reality. God's thoughts became reality because He spoke what He was thinking.

Seeds fulfill their potential as a result of being handled properly. All thoughts have potential reality! **The realities that we experience are simply the thoughts that we rehearse.** Jesus said, *"...out of the abundance of the heart the mouth speaketh."*[3] When Jesus speaks of the *heart* within this context, He is speaking of

4

the *soul* or *mind*. We all speak our predominant thoughts—what are YOU speaking? Start today the practice of saying only the thoughts that you want to see!

DAY 2

Think With Your Imagination

I have often said that we become what we imagine ourselves to be. Our focus today is on opening our thoughts to the miraculous realm of imagination.

God created us in His image and after His likeness. The image of God is in relation to His *form* or *figure,* while His likeness is described by His *function*. He gave form, function and a future to everything He created.

You did not ask, nor could you know how to ask, what your physical make-up would be: the color of your eyes, the shape of your nails, the size of your heart, tall, short, slim, not so slim. Everything about you was predetermined and perfectly formed by God. He created you exactly how He intended you to be. What is even more fantastic is that everything about you is a piece of Him!

The mistake so many of us make is falling into the trap of trading our original image for something that was not intended. This results in us becoming a caricature and not the character God designed us to be.

One definition of the word *thought* is the power to imagine. There is power in what you imagine. Your imagination replays your past and it pre-plays your future. See your imagination as a screen and begin to think through what you want it to display. Exercise your imagination daily. If you are like me, then you most likely had a huge imagination as a child and the screen got smaller as you grew older. I encourage you to find that place in your memory bank where you allowed yourself to dream big and begin to enlarge your screen again!

To see what we imagine ourselves becoming we must have a proper understanding of the image we are from. One companion to imagination is inspiration. Inspiration can cause you to believe in who you really are. It gives you the ability to see it and it ignites a passion to fulfill it. Your imagination allows you the fabulous luxury of thinking from the end—seeing yourself at the fulfillment of your purpose and intention—and there is no stopping anyone who can think from that end. **Your imagination has the power to form your future**.

Make a habit of spending time alone free from distractions and allow your mind to visualize the image of who you were created to be. These moments create opportunities for intimacy with our Creator. It is during these intimate moments that dreams are conceived and your imagination is put to work.

Dare to dream! This is a day to dream! This is a day to set your imagination free and see what God will say!

DAY 3

What Do You Think of Yourself?

Everyone desires significance. A major part of a person's significance is connected to their self-esteem. Whenever a person experiences a lack of respect, honor or gratitude, it directly affects a person's self-esteem. In turn, people who do not have proper self-esteem do not know how to show respect for others in a healthy way. Today's lesson will examine the importance of valuable thoughts concerning you.

The biblical passage, "…*as (a man) thinks… so is he*"[1] opens a new realm of consideration with regard to proper development. The connotation is not only *where* you see yourself, but also *how* you see yourself. As you are thinking, *how* are your thoughts concerning yourself? What is your estimation of yourself? Your estimation often predicts your expectation. I believe those who do not expect much of themselves have improper estimations about themselves.

Estimation is judging something in regards to its worth or its significance. If I own something and decide to sell it, I do not let the buyer determine its worth. There is a difference between relative worth and monetary worth. A price tag does not necessarily define the worth of a thing. It may cost everyone the same amount monetarily, but if one person needs it or desires it more than another, then there is a difference in the value of the same item.

Your worth is not in the mind or mouth of those around you. Your worth is what you determine it to be! Be deliberate in positive thoughts about yourself. **The best way for you to see yourself is to see you the way that God sees you**. You will gain a healthy perception by looking at yourself in the mirror of God's word:

Psalm 139:13-16[2] "*For you created my inmost being; you knit me together in my mother's womb. I praise you because I am fearfully and wonderfully made; your works are wonderful, I know that full well. My frame was not hidden from you when I was made in the secret place. When I was woven together in the depths of the earth, your eyes saw my unformed body. All the days ordained for me were written in your book before one of them came to be."*

When you find yourself in moments of doubt, insecurity or confusion, remind yourself that God sees you; He knows you and He made you. Enjoy the significance that comes from His perspective and acceptance of you. Practice thinking His thoughts concerning you!

DAY 4:

Think With Intention

Today we will learn how changing your mind can literally change your world! It is amazing that we are created with the ability to progressively enlarge our capacity of thought. We can train our minds to think in terms and levels that are larger than our present reality.

In order for your mind to operate in modes of larger living, there must be *intentional thinking*. God speaks through the prophet Jeremiah saying, "*For I know the thoughts **that I think** toward you, saith the LORD, thoughts of peace, and not of evil, to give you an expected end.*"[3]

Notice how *His thoughts* are interwoven into the fabric of *your life*. This is the pattern of destiny! The goal is success *or* an expected end. It suggests that God had and has *intentional thoughts* about you! We learned in chapter one that the omniscient God knew you before you were even formed and now continues to practice intentional thoughts about you. If this is the practice of the Source from which you were created, then I encourage you to duplicate that pattern in your own life.

This practice requires some discipline on your part. **Disciplines for success lead to the destiny of success**. Rather than entertaining every thought that comes into your mind, engage a thought out of your own intentions. This is a process and not an easy one at that. It takes time to build the discipline to intentionally produce quality thoughts—this is one of the distinguishing attributes between thinking purposefully and merely existing.

Once a quality thought is produced it must be captured. This is done through the process of rumination. One definition for the word *think* that comes from Hebrew culture is *to interpenetrate*. This interpretation describes the process of fully passing through a thing or permeating a thing. An example is to percolate or to cause a substance to pass through a filter over and over again.

Make time today to produce a purposeful thought. It may take work and your mind will likely want to wander into its usual pattern of thinking, but stay with your intention to find something new and purposeful for your life. Keep that image and train your mind to ruminate on it over and over until it has fully permeated your life.

"As nothing is more easy than to think, so nothing is more difficult than to think well."

— Thomas Traherne (c. 1637–1674) [4]

DAY 5

Where Do You Think Best?

I have learned that *where* I intentionally engage the practice of thinking is as important as *what* and *how* I am thinking. Today, let us focus our attention on the underestimated aspect of thinking: your surroundings.

There is a certain energy that flows at a different pace when you are doing something alone. The energy in the environment is as important as the energy you are expending in thought. **There are some environments that are more conducive than others for purposeful thinking**. Do you have a place that allows you to think productively and intentionally?

What works for me is walking. It allows me space and time to open my mind and think things through. I have a routine that I try to follow on a consistent basis—wake up, drink a bottle of water, then my coffee, and have a devotion/prayer time. Then I grab my walking shoes and dog leash and head out the door. Because I have made this a pattern, my mind seems to anticipate this time as a period for process and deliberation. Usually when my walk starts I allow my mind to wander, dream and think on happy places in my life, such as my grandchildren. From there I will remember something I have been working on or considering. Every time I walk there is some revelation, whether big or small, that becomes clearer to me. I am able to put things together in my mind that was once confusing or out of order.

Remember, your mind is a muscle. In your practice of thinking be deliberate about disengaging your mind from mentally exhausting distractions. Any personal trainer will preach the importance of not overworking your muscles in order to gain maximum growth and health. It is impossible to continuously push and stretch your body in every direction without experiencing fatigue. Even with the best of intentions for growth, many times we hinder ourselves by having our mind invested in too many places at once. Learn to give your mind a productive break.

Diversions work wonders for me. I have loved playing the guitar for most of my life. Everyday I find time to fool around on the guitar so I can pause and escape for a moment. That pause allows my mind to take a back seat to my heart and soul while I enjoy the muse of my guitar.

Hobbies can enhance your thought life. I encourage what Richard Exley calls, "*The rhythm of life*." The premise is to make deposits into four areas of life in order to maintain balance. These areas are—work, worship, rest and play. As a pastor, this is a principle that I have imparted into my congregation for many years. It is important to stress that there is a distinct difference between each of them.

I encourage you to take time today to contemplate *where* you find yourself practicing your thinking. It may be time to find new environments in which to think. A walk in the park, a drive alone, or just time outside—these offer you the opportunity to enhance your thoughts. In all your thinking…give your mind a break!

DAY 6

How You Think

A *paradigm* is the pattern or framework of thinking. It is why you think the way you think or why you see things as you see them. This is often the result of experiences that have transpired in your life. We filter thoughts through those events thus giving us a paradigm.

Jesus asked a question in the gospel of Matthew, "*How think ye?*"[3] **How you think will ultimately affect how you feel, and how you feel will directly influence how you function.** It is vitally important for us to always be cognizant of how we are thinking. It is the difference between the optimist and the pessimist.

Hopeful positive thinking produces a joyful bright outlook, which results in intentional action. Negative down-in-the-dump thinking produces a depressed hopeless outlook, which results in a lack of action or regretful action.

A *paradigm* is the framework of thinking, so we must frame our future by practicing positive thinking. The book of Hebrews tells us that, "...*the worlds were framed by the word of God.*"[3] The word *framed* has to do with adjusting or fitting out. If we continually renew our minds by God's Word then every aspect of life has to adjust to that Word. Your projection and protection is found in how you think.

Proverbs 4:23, "*Keep your heart with all diligence for out of it spring the issues of life.*"[1] Protecting your thinking is as important as anything you can do for your mind. There are patterns to follow that will you help with your paradigms.

One of the best practices is found in Philippians 4:8, "*Finally, brethren, whatsoever things are true, whatsoever things are honest, whatsoever things are just, whatsoever things are pure, whatsoever things are lovely, whatsoever things are of good report; if there be any virtue, and if there be any praise, think on these things.*"[3] Make this your pattern today!

DAY 7

Transformed Thinking

Romans 12:2, "*²And be not conformed to this world: but be ye transformed by the renewing of your mind, that ye may prove what is that good, and acceptable, and perfect, will of God.*"[3]

There are two words that stand out in this passage of scripture. The first is *conformed*. It has to do with being fashioned or following the same pattern—in reference to the world. The Apostle Paul is giving a stern warning concerning the time a man lives in. For every period of time there is call to conform. It is easy to get caught up in the currents and pulls of contemporary influence. It is much easier to fit in than it is to stand out.

Paul offers the remedy that is found in the word *transformed*. We must understand that being transformed happens as a result of a process. Transformation has to do with shaping something with the idea of adjusting the parts.

The Greek rendering of *transform* is where we get the word *metamorphosis*. It is a gradual structural adjustment. When we renew our minds there is a renovation procedure that occurs. If you have ever renovated a house, then you know that there is always demolition before construction. Renovations do not happen over night. They take time. **Therefore, in the practice of thinking, do not get discouraged if transforming your mind does not happen quickly—it is a process.**

Everyday we take another step in this process. The goal is transformation. Recognize that demolition *and* construction both represent progress. Make progress regardless of where you are in the process! Everyday presents the opportunity for transformation.

Think Before You Act

There is an old saying, "*Sow a thought and you reap an action, sow an action, reap a habit; sow a habit reap a character, sow a character reap a destiny.*"[5] I do believe that there is a certain truth to this. Somehow most of what happens with and through us begins with a thought. What goes in the mind will eventually come out —*I think, therefore I do, and therefore I am.* Our life is what our thoughts make us.

Destinies and lives that never fulfill their purpose are typically a result of a lack of *self-control.* In my opinion, this is one of the great tragedies of man. I firmly believe that the person who has no self-control is like a city without walls. That city has no defense. Self-control is really self-defense. The person with self-control is simply displaying thought-control. **If you can control your thoughts, then you can control your self.**

As we look again at Proverbs 23:7 it says, *"…
as he **thinketh** in his heart, so is he."*[3] The word
thinketh is a Hebrew verb, only found here,
and probably means, "As he is, all along in his
heart, so is he (at last) in act."

It is believed that the mind is so easily in-
fluenced that by looking at certain colors,
a person can be made to feel a certain way
and think certain thoughts. This is called the
priming effect. Be careful with your "eye-gates."
Jesus said the eye is the window to the soul.
What you look at long enough will become
what you think about.

Today, be careful with what you allow to get
into your mind. What are you looking at? What
has your attention? Remember that what you
dwell on you will ultimately live in!

DAY 9

Thinking With an Attitude

In 1910, Wallace D Wattles wrote his book "*The Science of Getting Rich*". A central part of the book is about thinking with a certain *attitude* regardless of circumstance. "*To think what you want to think is to think truth regardless of appearances. To think according to appearances is easy. To think truth regardless of appearances is laborious and requires the expenditure of more power than any other work you have to perform.*"[6] This requires the power of optimistic thinking.

There is something magnetic about optimistic people. They have a gravitational pull. In the same way, pessimistic people have a repelling force. **The attitude in which you think is *always* your decision**. How is your "*thought attitude*"? Is it negative? OR is it positive? What would others say? Are others encouraged by your optimistic attitude? Or do you discourage with pessimism?

Both optimism and pessimism can be contagious. Think about it—it is difficult to think positively in the midst of negative people. On the other hand it is difficult to think negatively in the midst of positive people. We all know that "*birds of a feather flock together*". Sometimes we need to change our *flock* in order to regain our optimism.

Martin Seligman says in his book, "*Learned Optimism*", "*Depression is nothing more than its symptoms. It is caused by conscious negative thoughts. There is no deep underlying disorder to be rooted out: not unresolved childhood conflicts, not our unconscious anger, and not even our brain chemistry.. Emotion comes directly from what we think: think "I am in danger and you feel anxiety, think I am being trespassed and you feel anger, think loss and you feel sadness… depression results from lifelong habits of conscious thought. If we change these habits of thought, we will cure depression.*"[7]

The power of positive thinking is irreplaceable. Sir Winston Churchill said, "*I am an optimist. It does not seem too much use being anything else.*" An *optimist* is a person who anticipates the best possible outcome of every circumstance. What matters the most is to make the best out of every situation. Be positive in your thoughts today! Have an optimistic attitude! Train your mind to be optimistic!

"Nothing can stop the man with the right mental attitude from achieving his goal; nothing on earth can help the man with the wrong mental attitude."[8]

- Thomas Jefferson

DAY 10

Wake Up Thinking Right

We live in a generation that is literally addicted to social media. We sleep with our phones plugged-in and sitting on a nightstand next to us. The first thing most of us do when we wake up is look at social media, their texts, email or some other news feed. We cannot wait to see the number of likes we received on a post or picture and then we begin reading or watching what others have posted. The problem with this behavioral pattern is that we are subjecting ourselves to others thoughts and opinions. These opinions are usually troublesome and trivial. Sadly many times this is how we start our day.

The principle of *"first"* is a Biblical principle that simply means *the first sets the pattern for the rest.* In the gospel of Matthew, Jesus said, *"Seek... FIRST the Kingdom... and His righteousness; and all these things shall be added to (us)."*[3] There is also the *"law of first mentioned"* that suggests that what God says the first time about any subject in scripture is the basis for other reasoning concerning that subject. In other words, the *first* is the blueprint or design.

While I was raising and training horses on my ranch, I learned the benefit of getting my hands on newborn colts. In horse training this is called *first impression*. By lightly touching, holding and putting my hands all over the young colts it caused them to accept my hands later in their life as full-grown horses. They never forgot the *first impression*. First impressions always stay in someone's mind. They have a lasting effect. This often creates an opinion or mental image of someone or something that is hard to change. There is a reason that God *says* things first *and does* things first—He knows the power of *first impressions*.

What is the first thing you think about when you wake up? What is the first thing that you do? In scripture David writes, "*Early will I seek You* (God)." I believe he understood the principle of the first and applied it to his daily life.

Your first thought *of* **the day more than likely will be your predominant thought** *for* **the day**. Develop a daily practice (first thing every morning) to set your mind on your purpose and be conscious of what unfolds next!

DAY 11

Think Before You Speak

The pathway from mind to mouth must be constructed with yield signs and stop signs—in some cases detour signs. Some of the things that people say certainly show that there is not much quality thought behind their talk.

Is it true that some things we say actually "*slip out of our mouth*"? Yes, it is true. A slip of the tongue means we thought it and spoke it without capturing it and considering its effect. We are accountable for what we say. Your thoughts are made known when you speak. Therefore, you are judged by what comes out of your mouth. If you want to know what people are thinking just listen to what they say!

The build-up of thought will create an overflow that evolves into a language. Remember, you do not have to say everything you think. **Learning to *say* the things that you want to *see* is imperative if you want those things to manifest in your life.** Whatever you say (over and over) you will ultimately see. Say what you want to see and learn to speak the *positive* things you think.

As you go through your day hear yourself saying what you are about to say before you say it. Assess it and determine if the thought is worthy of words. Announce quality thoughts and it will produce quality results!

DAY 12:

The Rehearsal of Thought

"You are what you repeatedly do. Excellence is not an event - it is a habit"[10]

What we repeatedly practice we will ultimately become good at. This is also true of living a victorious life. There is a reason that God told Moses in Exodus 17 to rehearse things in the ears of Joshua, *"And the LORD said unto Moses, Write this for a memorial in a book, and* **rehearse it** *in the ears of Joshua: for I will utterly put out the remembrance of Amalek from under heaven."*[3] To *rehearse* is to practice over and over in private (your mind) before public performance. The product of practice is a better performance.

It has been proven that mental practice tends to separate the great from the average. A receiver in football will close his eyes and visualize his routes or patterns until they are forged in his mind. Musicians will close their eyes and play scales or songs in their mind until it is easy to recall. In other words, there is growing evidence that mental practice (if done correctly) can absolutely make a difference in one's performance. A key to producing quality results in life is to develop a process of thinking that is repeated until it becomes second nature.

I recently read from a website called sports-training-adviser.com that *mental* practice is the cognitive rehearsal of a physical skill without movement. It is effective both for learning skills and preparing for competition. Sport psychologists often use visualizations and rehearsal to help motivate, to build self-confidence and to reduce competitive anxiety.

What we repeatedly think about we will ultimately accomplish. What thoughts do you rehearse? Rehearse thoughts of yourself excelling, winning and succeeding! The thoughts you rehearse are the ones that will become second nature and reality in your everyday life.

DAY 13

Thinking Ahead

As a young man my dad taught me the value of *thinking ahead*. He was a pipeline welder and would hire me as a welder helper. If I was not working for him, I was helping a brother, a brother-in-law or a cousin. They were all welders and always needed a helper. The most important thing to them was *time*. I cannot describe how often they emphasized these words, "*Think ahead! I do not want to be waiting on you.*" This meant I had to always be one-step ahead of them. They did not tolerate having to wait on me to prepare materials for when they arrived at the next weld.

Thinking ahead is the ability to see what is coming and prepare for it. To *think ahead* means to think carefully about what might happen in the future or to make plans for things you want to do in the future.

In my opinion this practice works best with predictability. You cannot think ahead for unforeseen events, but it is easy to think ahead about things that are inevitable. What is routine and regimented in our life could become much easier if we planned for them before they arrived.

In the book of Proverbs chapter six there is an illustration concerning thinking ahead. It reads:

"You lazy fool, look at an ant. Watch it closely; let it teach you a thing or two. Nobody has to tell it what to do. All summer it stores up food; at harvest it stockpiles provisions. So how long are you going to laze around doing nothing? How long before you get out of bed? A nap here, a nap there, a day off here, a day off there, sit back, take it easy—do you know what comes next? Just this: You can look forward to a dirt-poor life, poverty your permanent houseguest!"[9]

In my preaching I have always followed this thought; "*I study myself full, I pray myself hot, I THINK myself happy, and I let myself go.*" It produces a consistency in my preaching in spite of the variables that may arise.

Think ahead today! What are the things that you know this day holds for you? Think ahead on how you can better prepare for them to arrive. Understand that there will always be unforeseen circumstances. How will you respond to these potential circumstances—whether they are obstacles, delays or changes of direction? **Thinking ahead prepares you for optimum performance!**

DAY 14

Thoughts and Emotions

There is an emotional charge attached to every thought. Every thought is pulling you toward or away from a certain emotion. The closest thing to neutral thought is entertainment (amusement), but even then you are thinking about what you are watching or doing.

Have you ever been sitting with someone and watched their visage change as they were caught in a daze? Then you ask, "*What are you thinking about?*" Something sparked a thought, and they tracked that thought until it touched an emotion, and the emotion manifested in an expression. I truly believe that a disengaged mind will tend toward the feeling of emptiness. The feeling of emptiness lends itself towards emotional depression.

What we process in our mind becomes the product of our life. Recently I experienced this. A few blood tests caused my doctor to be concerned about my health. He relayed those concerns to me and I found myself continually thinking the worst. My thinking about the worst in turn produced depressed emotions. Ultimately my doctor ordered a test that would bring clarity and definitive answers concerning my health. When the results showed that my health was intact, I felt very different. This one report completely changed my emotional state of being because it caused me to see and therefore think differently.

If you want productive, peaceful and purposeful days of enjoyment then you must be aware of what thoughts you are engaged with. Practice intentional thinking. Think thoughts that produce and lend themselves to positive emotions. Do not allow whatever comes your way to be the force that pulls you in uncertain directions. **Ultimately, you are the one who decides your emotional state of being!** *Think about it...*

Think Your Way to Perfect Peace

Throughout scripture the Lord has proven to be a God of pattern and design. Whether it be for Noah to build an Ark or Moses to build a Tabernacle, God always gave a blueprint to men He could trust. He is such a loving and caring God that He chooses not to control us, but to allow us to think and live according to our own will. However, He loves us so much that He gives us direction and encourages us to follow that leading.

In relation to our thinking—He gives us powerful patterns to follow that result in a successful state of being. The prophet Isaiah states, *"Thou wilt keep* **him** *in perfect peace,* **whose** *mind* **is** *stayed* **on thee**: *because he trusteth in thee."*[(3)]

Remember that your paradigm of thinking is your framework or *pattern* of thought. It is why you see a thing the way you see it. We have the potential and ability to frame our thinking by capturing our thought patterns. The phrase, *"whose mind is stayed on thee…"* has the connotation of leaning on Him or taking hold of him. Think about it—we do not lean on what we do not trust to hold us up. The Proverb says, *"…lean not on your own understanding; in all your ways acknowledge Him…."*[1] Are you trusting in your own ability to direct your own life? OR are you leaning on God to hold you up and direct your steps?

The power of right thinking brings a life of perfect peace. **There is no one exempt from troubled times, but troubled times do not exempt peace from being available to the one who keeps his mind on trusting God.** Perfect peace is a state of safety, the feeling of being happy and in a secure place.

Allow God to be your shelter of peace today. Keep your mind on Him and you will be kept in perfect peace!

Defeat Fearful Thinking

Fearful thoughts can hold us hostage and cause us to never progress in our God-given purpose. Fear is something that tries to take up residence in our minds. If it finds a place to abide it will capture your thoughts and paralyze you.

There are many different fears that people battle with. The fear of failure is a very common fear. It is closely related to the fear of criticism and the fear of rejection. The fear of failure as it applies to the achievement of a goal, could be defined as an emotion aroused when we believe that a certain desired outcome is unattainable. This is one of the greatest fears people struggle with. In order to attain success you must overcome the fear of failure.

The Law of Feedback states: there is no failure; there is only feedback. Successful people look at mistakes as outcomes or results, not as failure. Unsuccessful people look at mistakes as permanent and personal.

Most people limit themselves. Most people do not achieve a fraction of what they are capable of achieving—they are afraid to try because they are afraid to fail.

There are three other types of fear I feel are vitally important to understand—learned fear, associated fear, and acquired fear. These fears are lethal to our progress and we must be aware when we are dealing with one. To best define them I will give an example of how they manifest.

Learned Fear - You entered a music competition as a child and lost. This loss may have caused you to develop a fear of contests. This is a directly *learned* fear.

Associated Fear - You may have become a very gifted poet, but because of the fear you developed fifteen years earlier from losing the music competition, you now choose to not submit your poetry in a writers contest. You have an *associated* fear of *all* contests because of your earlier experience even though you have never entered a writing contest. You will not enter any form of competition despite the fact that you have now developed confidence and have established credibility as a gifted poet.

Acquired Fear - Imagine that you continued your life with this fear of contests. Now imagine you have a family with children. Suppose you teach your children to avoid contests or competitive events because of your *learned* and *associated* fears. Given the circumstances, they may have a fear of contests without ever entering a competition of any kind. This is called *acquired* fear.

It is impossible to think correctly yet simultaneously allow fear to have a predominant place in your thoughts. When you think about the will of God for your life, it removes all fear from your mind. Learn to overcome thoughts of fear with the thoughts of God's love for you!

I John 4:18, "*¹⁸There is no fear in love; but perfect love casteth out fear: because fear hath torment. He that feareth is not made perfect in love.*"[3]

The Message Bibles states it like this—*"There is no room in love for fear. Well-formed love banishes fear. Since fear is crippling, a fearful life—fear of death, fear of judgment—is one not yet fully formed in love."*[9]

Remove fear from your thoughts today!

"Failure is only the opportunity to begin again more intelligently"[11]

- Henry Ford

The Think Bank

You may remember the movie, "Total Recall." It was about a man who after seeing an ad from Rekall, buys an imaginary adventure by receiving implants of *false memories*.

Confabulation is the formation of false memories, perceptions, or beliefs about the self or the environment as a result of neurological or psychological dysfunction.

When it is a matter of memory, confabulation is the confusion of *imagination* with *memory*, or the *confused application of true memories*.

Simply put, when your memory is damaged and replaced by false imaging, your future becomes an adventure that is orchestrated by what others design and impart in your brain without your permission.

Our memory bank is filled with events, experiences and encounters that left impressions in our mind. Some of them are victorious while others are debilitating. When we recall certain and particular times it leaves us with either a feeling of happiness or sadness. Sometimes we give certain recollections more potency and credence than they should *actually* have by confusing what actually happened. The enemy loves nothing more than for your negative memories to be confabulated and false thoughts concerning yourself established in your mind.

In every web browser there is a "history". If you would like to know what someone has been looking at on the Internet, you look at the history of their browser. There is also a "delete" option or a "clear all history" option that will wipe out the history of the browser.

I encourage you to go through your memory bank today. **Make a withdrawal and dispose of the cluttered memories that cause unnecessary stress, confusion, or pain.** Allow God to delete the history of failure, mistakes and shortcomings from your mind today. He is faithful and just to forgive us and to *cleanse* us from all iniquity. Begin to make strong *positive* deposits into your memory bank. Let recent and real time victories supersede old and out-of-date negative memories. Put something positive in the bank today!

"Memory is the cabinet of imagination, the treasury of reason,

the registry of conscience, and the council chamber of thought."

- Saint Basil (c. 330–379) [12]

DAY 18

Clarity of Thought

Someone once said, "*Focus is one of the most necessary ingredients of character and one of the best instruments of success. Without focus creativity wastes its efforts in a maze of inconsistencies.*"[(13)]

Focus is a state or condition that permits clear understanding or perception. It is important to remember that perception is what you see as a result of your understanding. Therefore, focus is directly tied to perception. It is very difficult to focus on things that we do not understand and it is just as difficult to understand things you do not put focus on.

When my thinking is focused I tend to be more productive. An unfocused mind that is constantly allowed to meander is a mind that is distracted from destiny. In the book of Hebrews the writer uses the phrases "*fix your eyes*" and "*Look unto Jesus*". *Fixing your eyes* on something is focusing on that thing with all of your attention. When we consider something attentively or discern it clearly we are in the mode of focus.

Many times we have to look away from certain things in order to look at other things. There are so many opportunities to be distracted in your thinking. So many things want your attention. When you try to give attention to everything at once, then nothing is completed. It is impossible to completely focus on everything and be successful, but you *must* focus on something. Focus will always fortify your faith and remove doubt.

There has to be a point of concentration. **Something will be the center of your attention and you are the one that determines what that *something* is.** Do not allow your thinking to be clouded or crowded with voices and visuals that pull you in vain directions. Focus on what counts! It is more valuable to think and focus on your future (where you are going) than it is to focus your past (where you were). You cannot allow past mistakes to keep your thinking locked in a cycle. Your past must not be allowed to dictate your future.

Focus refers to *adjustment for clear vision* as well as *the field of clear vision*, and it has a geometrical definition of a fixed point. Minor adjustments go a long way when it comes to focusing our thinking.

What adjustments can you make today that will bring clarity to your paradigm? I encourage you to fix your focus today!

"We see actual things, and we say that we see them, but we never really see them until we see God; when we see God, everything becomes different. It is not the external things that are different, but a different disposition looks through the same eyes as the result of the internal surgery that has taken place."

- Oswald Chambers[14]

The Art of Thinking

Meditation is the art of thinking. Christian leaders rarely speak about it, but it is a subject that is not overlooked in scripture. We find early on that Joshua is encouraged to practice meditation. Joshua was told that if he did, there would be a guaranty of enjoying a prosperous and successful life.

In the book of Joshua the first chapter reads, *"This book of the law shall not depart out of thy mouth; but* **thou shalt meditate therein day and night**, *that thou mayest observe to do according to all that is written therein: for then thou shalt make thy way prosperous, and then thou shalt have good success."*[3]

Meditation defined in this instance is *the act of focusing one's thoughts: to ponder, think on, or to muse.* To *muse* is very interesting because it not only means deep consideration, but it is also the root word for music. Many biblical teachers believe meditation in Hebrew had an association with sound—specifically music.

Some of the best times of meditation for me are those that are enhanced by music. So while I may be hearing music, I am not really focused on it. Music creates an incredible atmosphere for meditation. **Something that soothes the soul brings a certain ambience to thinking peaceful thoughts.**

Meditation will move you to realms of living a prosperous life. I am not referring to a bank account full of money. The prosperous life I am referring to has to do with pushing forward and breaking out of ruts and cycles that are detrimental to your destiny. The promise to Joshua, I believe, is the promise to all of us. You will begin to walk in success when you begin to meditate on favorable and desired outcomes.

Someone said, "*Some people think that meditation takes time away from physical accomplishment. Taken to extremes, of course, that's true. Most people, however, find that meditation creates more time than it takes.*"[15]

"Plant the seed of meditation and reap the fruit of peace of mind." [16]

Hear are some Psalms to meditate on today-

Psalms 5:1-3**,** *Give ear to my words, O LORD, consider* **my meditation***. Hearken unto the voice of my cry, my King, and my God: for unto thee will I pray.* [3]

Psalms 1:2, *But his delight is in the law of the LORD, and in His law he meditates day and night.* [3]

Psalms 4:4, *Tremble, and do not sin; Meditate in your heart upon your bed, and be still.* [3]

Psalms 19:14, *Let the words of my mouth, and* **the meditation of my heart***, be acceptable in thy sight, O LORD, my strength, and my redeemer.* [3]

Think On These Things

Yesterday we considered meditation. Today I would like us to focus on *eight directors of thought*. When these eight ingredients become the drivers of our thought process and the focus of our meditation, the result is peace, productivity and a positive outlook on life. Let's dive in.

Philippians 4:8-9 - *⁸Finally, brethren, whatsoever things are true, whatsoever things are honest, whatsoever things are just, whatsoever things are pure, whatsoever things are lovely, whatsoever things are of good report; if there be any virtue, and if there be any praise, think on these things. ⁹Those things, which ye have both learned, and received, and heard, and seen in me, do: and the God of peace shall be with you.* (2)

Let's look at each director succinctly. Ask yourself how close you are to following these leads.

1. True – not concealed.

When something is true you will find that it is loyal and in accordance with reality.

Thinking in modes of truth has a certain authenticity to it. It does not waste time fantasizing. Do not think on things that are hidden, *things about which you are ignorant.* If it is not genuine and real, why allow it to take up residence in your mind?

2.   Honest

This kind of thinking is honorable thinking. It is free from fraud and deception. We could compare this kind of thinking to how we think about people. Are your thoughts concerning people filled with integrity?

3.   Just

Equitable thinking has a mind that is ruled by principle. Principle based thinking cements your convictions and cannot be negotiable. If you compromise your thinking you jeopardize your future.

4.   Pure

This kind of thinking is clean, innocent or modest. In the time that we inhabit, this can be a challenging discipline. If thoughts are not pure then life is not pure.

5.   Lovely

Lovely thoughts are thoughts that are friendly towards someone, specifically the person that you are attached to in life. Be careful; do not get caught in a trap of negative thinking towards those you are attached to. Find lovely thoughts about those you are attached to (i.e. spouse, children, parents) and magnify them in your mind.

6.   Good Report

Be cautious; watch what you entertain about others from people who are anxious to tell you the bad. Reputable thinking only considers what is GOOD. This means we do not allow rumors or gossip to run laps in our mind.

7.   Virtue

This has to do with valor or intrinsic excellence. Think on things that provide strength—the kind of strength that gives a lift. Uplifting thoughts promote a life that ascends to excellence.

8.   Praise

Praise thinking is simply positive and uplifting thoughts—thoughts that are worthy of praise.

The praise thought must be something that God would be pleased to hear.

Take inventory of your thoughts today. Ask yourself how your thoughts line up with these eight directors. Make a conscious effort to "… *take captive every thought and make them obedient to Christ.*"[2]

PHIL. 4:8-9, (Message Bible) [8]*Summing it all up, friends, I'd say you'll do best by filling your minds and meditating on things true, noble, reputable, authentic, compelling, gracious - the best, not the worst; the beautiful, not the ugly; things to praise, not things to curse.* [9]*Put into practice what you learned from me, what you heard and saw and realized. Do that, and God, who makes everything work together, will work you into his most excellent harmonies.*[9]

DAY 21

Another Level of Thinking

The same level of thinking that got you where you are may not take you where you want to go. We have all heard the phrase "*think outside the box.*" That is a very good approach to enlarging your thoughts. However, there is another term I like to use, "*think on another level*". Scripture often encourages us to lift our eyes or to look up, insinuating that there is a lift provided that you can enjoy. It is thinking on a higher plain!

I want to conclude our devotion in considering Proverbs 24:3-4, which states, "*³It takes wisdom to build a house, and understanding to set it on a firm foundation; ⁴It takes knowledge to furnish its rooms with fine furniture and beautiful draperies.*"[9] In this passage from the Bible there is a progression of thought.

First of all, *wisdom builds.* Wisdom is the highest level of thought. Wisdom is as infinite as God himself. As we increase in it, it increases in us. As we grow in wisdom we advance in favor. Pray for God to give you wisdom and take your thinking to the next level.

Secondly, there is *understanding*. Jesus said, what we understand cannot be taken from us. The Apostle Paul said, that understanding establishes us and we see that in this proverb— understanding is connected to the foundation. In order to have understanding you must make an effort such as this scripture encourages:

Proverbs 2:1-2, "*¹My son, if thou wilt receive my words, and hide my commandments with thee; ²So that thou incline thine ear unto wisdom, and apply thine heart to understanding;*"⁽³⁾

Understanding is the ability to see how every event in life has to do with a far greater picture. This is called comprehension. I believe that understanding is really revelation. *Revelation* is comprehending something for the first time that you have looked at for a long time.

Lastly, *knowledge fills*. Knowledge is information that comes from education. It fills your mind with options for you to think about. We can only draw from what we have learned.

A wise person has the confluence of knowledge and understanding at work in them. It is the applying what you both know and understand within the framework of wisdom.

Think higher thoughts today. Challenge yourself to think on a higher level! **Seek wisdom, walk in understanding and *know* in your thoughts that all things are working for you!**

Conclusion

My prayer is that the last 21 days have been encouraging, enlightening and empowering. I pray that as you continue to put these ideas and principles of thought into practice, that your life would be productive, full of joy and fulfillment.

I encourage you to go through this 21-day process of mental discipline periodically throughout the year. If you do, I assure that you will experience transformation and enjoy the abundant and fruitful life that Christ promised you.

Bibliography

1. New King James Version®. Copyright © 1982 by Thomas Nelson.
2. Holy Bible, New International Version®, NIV® Copyright ©1973, 1978, 1984, 2011 by Biblica, Inc.®
3. Holy Bible, King James Version. Public Domain.
4. Quote by Thomas Traherne (c. 1637–1674)
5. Quote by Ralph Waldo Emerson
6. Wattles, Wallace D. "The Science of Getting Rich" Elizabeth Towne Company, 1910
7. Seligman, Martin E. P. "Learned Optimism" New York: Vintage Books, 1990
8. Quote by Thomas Jefferson
9. Peterson, Eugene H. "The Message Bible" NavPress Publishing Group, 1993
10. Quote by Will Durant
11. Quote by Henry Ford
12. Quote by Saint Basil (c. 330–379)
13. Mason, John "You're Born an Original (Don't Die A Copy)" Insight International, 1993
14. Chambers, Oswald "Not Knowing Whither: The Steps of Abraham's Faith" Oswald Chambers Publications Association, Limited, 1934
15. Quote by Peter McWilliams
16. Quote by Remez Sasson

Other Books by Rick Hawkins

The Wall: Disaster or Destiny?

Lessons from Life's Crossroads.

The Inner Circle

The Value of Friendship, Trust & Influence

The Benjamin Blessing

God's Five-Fold Plan for Your Destiny

www.rickhawkins.org

μ65

Powered by eGenco

Generation Culture Transformation
Specializing in publishing for generation culture change

Visit us Online at:
www.micro65.com

Write to: eGenco
824 Tallow Hill Road
Chambersburg, PA 17202, USA
Phone: 717-461-3436
Email: info@micro65.com

facebook.com/egenbooks
youtube.com/egenpub
egen.co/blog
twitter.com/egen_co
instagram.com/egen.co